FOOD AND CELEBRATIONS
JAPAN

Sylvia Goulding

WAYLAND

This edition published in 2008 by Wayland
(a division of Hachette Children's Books)

Wayland
Hachette Children's Books
338 Euston Road
London NW1 3BH

Wayland Australia
Level 17/207 Kent Street
Sydney NSW 2000

© 2008 The Brown Reference Group plc

The Brown Reference Group plc
First Floor
9–17 St. Albans Place
London N1 0NX
www.brownreference.com

ISBN-13: 978-0-750256-39-1

Printed in Dubai

Wayland is a division of Hachette Children's Books,
an Hachette Livre UK Company.
www.hachettelivre.co.uk

10 9 8 7 6 5 4 3 2 1

Photographic Credits:
Front Cover: Shutterstock (inset); Klaus Arras (main)
Back Cover: Klaus Arras
Alamy: LMR Group 6, fStop 24; **iStock:** title page, 3, 41;
Paula Keogh: 7, 9, 13, 36; **Shutterstock:** 1, 3, 4, 5, 7,
8, 10, 12, 16, 19, 20, 22, 23, 28, 30, 31, 35, 38, 39, 40.

With thanks to models:
Caspar, Mariam, Miho, and Nils

Cooking Editor
Angelika Ilies has always been interested in cookery
and other countries. She studied nutritional sciences
in college. She has lived in the United States, England
and Germany. She has also travelled extensively and
collected international recipes on her journeys.
Angelika has written more than 70 cookbooks and
cooking card series. She currently lives in Frankfurt,
Germany, with her two children and has spent much
time researching children's nutrition. Both children
regularly cook with their mother.

Project Editor: Sylvia Goulding
Cooking Editor: Angelika Ilies
Contributors: Jacqueline Fortey, Sylvia Goulding
Photographers: Klaus Arras, Lucy Suleiman
Cartographer: Darren Awuah
Art Editor: Paula Keogh
Illustrator: Jo Gracie
Picture Researcher: Mike Goulding
Managing Editor: Bridget Giles
Production Director: Alastair Gourlay
Editorial Director: Lindsey Lowe
Children's Publisher: Anne O'Daly

Contents

let's START COOKING

Cooking is fun – you learn about different ingredients and cooking methods, you find out how things taste, and you can serve a meal to your family and friends that you have cooked yourself! Some of the recipes in this book have steps that need adult help – ask a parent or other adult if they will be your kitchen assistant while you cook a meal.

This line tells you how many people the meal will feed.

In this box, you find out which ingredients you need for your meal.

WHAT YOU NEED:

SERVES 4 PEOPLE:

500g white rice
4 eggs, beaten
light soy sauce
4 tablespoons
   groundnut
   or soya oil
2 spring onions
50g peeled prawns
50g ham
50g peas

Check before you start that you have everything at home. If something is missing, write it on your shopping list. Get all the ingredients ready before you start cooking.

◁ One of the great things about cooking is that you get to taste all the food first. That helps your cooking skills, too. You learn how to make it all taste better

! WHEN TO GET help

Most cooking involves cutting ingredients and heating them in some way, whether frying, boiling or cooking in the oven. Each time you see this exclamation mark, be extra careful as you cook, and make sure your adult kitchen assistant is around to help.

For many meals you need to chop vegetables into small strips. Wash all the vegetables first. Trim off any parts that are starting to wilt or turn yellow. Cut off any stems, peel the vegetables, and scrape out seeds, if there are any. Cut the good parts of the vegetables into fine strips. Try and cut all the strips into similar lengths and shapes so that they cook evenly.

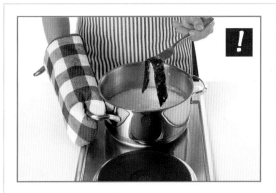

Nori and other seaweeds are featured in many Japanese dishes. Boil the seaweed in a saucepan of water, and leave it to bubble for about 2 minutes. Lift the seaweed out of the pan. When it is cool enough to handle, cut it into the shape you need with scissors. You can also cut or crumble it into small pieces and add it to soups and other dishes as a garnish. Some seaweed is sold as flakes.

Chopsticks are tools that Japanese people use instead of knives and forks to eat their food. It is fun to try using them.

Japanese **table settings** are very stylish. People often use square plates. The plates might be black, white or red.

To make sushi, Japanese people use a **sushi rolling mat**. The mat is usually made from bamboo sticks.

A **tea whisk** is one of many tools people use for the Japanese tea ceremony. It is used to whisk up the tea paste.

A trip around
JAPAN

Japan is a fascinating country full of contrasts. It has modern hi-tech cities as well as traditional customs. Its food is among the best in the world.

Japan is an island state. It consists of four main islands and more than 4,000 smaller ones. The country lies in the Pacific Ocean. It is separated from the east coasts of China and Russia by the Sea of Japan. Japan's land area is a bit more than the whole of the British Isles.

Japan has many mountains and active volcanoes. Its fast-flowing rivers have carried soil from the mountains to form fertile plains along the coast. These plains now make up most of Japan's farming land. Japan has hot, wet summers and cold, dry winters.

Japan has about 127 million inhabitants. Most live in crowded cities along the coast. The capital is Tokyo. Other important cities are Yokohama, Osaka, Nagoya, Sapporo and Kobe.

Ring of Fire

Japan lies in the Pacific Ring of Fire. This is an arc-shaped line around the Pacific Ocean where many volcanoes and earthquakes occur. Earth's crust is made of huge plates that meet in places such as the Pacific Ring of Fire.

These plates are moving, which can cause earthquakes and make volcanoes erupt. Japan has about 200 volcanoes and nearly one-third are active. People in Japan have to build houses and office buildings that can survive earthquakes. They also use early warning systems.

The official language of Japan is Japanese. Many people also understand and speak some English. The main religions in Japan are Shinto and Buddhism.

◁ **Japan** is in north-eastern Asia. It has four large and more than 4,000 small islands. Its nearest mainland neighbours are Russia, Korea and China.

ASIA
AFRICA
JAPAN

2

◁ **Japan's mountains**, such as the Zao range, are often covered in snow and ideal for skiing. There are also crater lakes, more than 100 hot springs, and superb scenery.

CHINA

RUSSIA

3

HOKKAIDO
● Sapporo

SEA OF JAPAN
(EAST SEA)

1

2

JAPAN

HONSHU
TOKYO

△ **Kyushu Island** is in the south of Japan. It has mild winters. At the south of the island, coral reefs attract divers. Inland, there are many hot springs, fertile valleys and mountain ranges.

5

Kyoto
Kobe ●
Hiroshima ●   ● Nagoya
● Osaka

SHIKOKU

1

△ **Tokyo**, Japan's capital city, has low-lying areas, high mountains and even some volcanic islands within its city limits.

5

Nagasaki
●
KYUSHU

3

PACIFIC
OCEAN

4

◁ **This floating torii** marks the entrance to a sacred site, the Shinto Itsukushima Shrine near Hiroshima.

▷ **The Ring of Fire** is an area around the edges of the Pacific Ocean. Earthquakes and volcanic eruptions are a constant danger to cities nearby.

4

Hokkaido Island

Hokkaido is Japan's most northern and second largest island. Here, the summers are warm and the winters long and harsh. It has many mountains, with lakes and rivers, and lowlands near the coasts. Visitors come to ski in winter, or to visit its national parks and underground hot-water springs.

Honshu Island

Honshu is Japan's largest island, so it is also called the mainland. Most people live here. More than twelve million people live in Tokyo, the bustling capital. With its suburbs and surroundings, the city is one of the most populated cities on Earth.

The Japanese Alps sweep down the centre of Honshu Island. Mount Fuji (3,776m) is an extinct volcano near the capital. It is famous for its beautiful shape and snow-covered top, and is the country's national symbol. Nearly 500km west of Tokyo is Lake Biwa, Japan's largest freshwater lake.

▽ **Mount Fuji** is Japan's highest mountain and an extinct volcano, so it will no longer erupt. Its summit is often shrouded in clouds and mist, making it hard to see.

△ **Heian Jingu** in Kyoto is one of more than 90,000 Shinto shrines in Japan. Shinto is Japan's main religion. Many Shinto shrines look like Buddhist temples, and they are often coloured red. Each temple has a gate, called a *torii*.

Shikoku Island

Shikoku is separated from Honshu by the Inland Sea, which is dotted with small islands. The islands are linked by several long bridges. Shikoku has mountains in the centre and coral reefs on its south-western coast. The climate is mild, but it is rainy and stormy in summer.

Kyushu Island

Kyushu has broad plains and steep mountains. Mount Aso (1,592m), Japan's tallest active volcano, is here. On the western side, near the city of Nagasaki, lie the Unzen volcanoes. From time to time, deadly flows of hot gas and rock sweep down into the valleys. But the volcanoes also provide spectacular scenery, fertile volcanic soil and health-giving hot springs. Kyushu's cities and its farms are in the west.

Okinawa

Okinawa is a region. It includes three island groups and stretches for 960km south-west of Kyushu. Okinawa Island has superb beaches, caves and small fishing villages. The seas around the southern islands contain coral reefs that teem with fish and other sealife.

SHAKY GROUND

On average, Japan has three minor earthquakes every day. The worst happened in 1923; 100,000 people died. An earthquake in Kobe in 1995 killed 6,000 people and destroyed 285,000 homes.

The food we grow in
JAPAN

Only a small part of the Japanese countryside can be farmed, but its coasts provide plenty of food.

Mountains and swamplands dominate large stretches of land, so cultivation is limited to the low-lying valleys and plains. Here water-loving plants, such as rice, thrive.

Northern farms

Hokkaido is Japan's most important island for growing food. It has large dairy farms that produce milk and cheese. Animals are reared for beef, pork and mutton. Crops grown in the north include rice, potatoes, barley, beans, cabbages and onions, as well as apples and pears. Soba (buckwheat) from here is used to make the world-famous soba noodles.

Hokkaido is also known for its fish and seafood. Crab in particular is prized for its excellent flavour. Scallops, sea urchins, salmon, herring, plaice, cod, squid, octopus, prawns, abalone and kelp are also collected.

Mainland crops

On Honshu Island the landscape is rugged, so most crops are grown on the lower hillsides and flat ground. Rice farmers grow medium-grain rice in wet, muddy fields called paddies.

THIRTY-A-DAY

Japanese people eat more than fish, soybeans and rice. In fact, children are taught to eat 30 different foods a day, and 100 a week!

◁ **Green tea** is grown at the foot of Mount Fuji. Together with tea from Kyoto, it is considered among the best. Green tea is such a popular drink that people only speak of 'tea' or 'Japanese tea'. Green tea is never drunk with milk or sugar.

Rice is Japan's main food. It is prepared in both swee and savoury dishes. After cooking, the rice grains stick together, which makes it ideal for sushi.

Honshu has vast plantations of green tea. Juicy oranges do well along the warm coast of the Inland Sea. The soya beans, or *edamame*, that grow here are made into many different soy sauces and into a beancurd called tofu.

Mainland livestock

Most beef cattle are farmed in the west of Honshu Island. The world-famous and expensive Kobe beef is made from black Wagyu cattle, which came originally from the port of Kobe. Farmers also keep dairy cows to supply milk to large cities. Pigs are raised all over Japan.

The South

The climate in Kyushu and Shikoku is mild, and the winters on the Pacific coast are warm. Farmers grow rice, sweet potatoes, cucumbers, aubergines, peppers, sugarcane, mandarin oranges, peaches, persimmons, grapes, lemons, bananas and beans. Herds of beef cattle graze in Kyushu's pastures, and farmers keep poultry for eggs and meat.

On Shikoku's eastern plains, cereals grow well. Some southern areas produce two crops of rice, wheat and barley a year. Farmers also

▽ **Pigs are raised** all over Japan, and pork is a popular meat. It is eaten as cutlets, minced in dumplings, cold as pork shabu shabu, in stir-fries, in a sweet and sour sauce or boiled.

grow vegetables and fruit under plastic so they can be harvested early. But many people from Shikoku and other rural parts of Japan are leaving the countryside. They are moving to the cities in search of work.

Fishing

Japan has one of the world's largest fishing fleets. Its trawlers net large amounts of fish in the deep sea. Local fishermen catch fish from shallow waters along Japan's long coastlines. Hokkaido's waters produce catches of herring, cod, halibut and squid. The catches have been smaller in recent years, so more fish are now imported from other countries. Freshwater fish farms raise trout and salmon, and seawater fish farms raise prawns, sea bream and seaweed.

Japan's most popular delicacies – sushi and sashimi – are made with raw fish. In the large fishing ports, such as Hachinhohe in north-eastern Honshu, huge catches of fish can be frozen, stored and processed so the fish gets to market fresh from the sea.

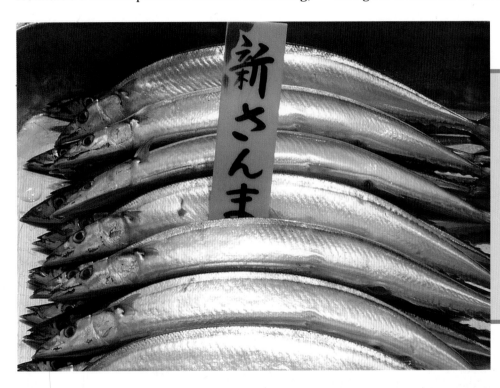

Fish for sale at Tsukiji fish market in Tokyo. This fish market is one of the largest in the world. It handles more than 400 types of fish, shellfish and seaweed. You can buy anything from tiny sardines to 260-kilo tuna.

THE SECRET OF A LONG LIFE

The people of Okinawa are known to reach old age – on average just over 90 years. Scientists think the secret of their success is an active life as fishermen and farmers and their healthy diet.

let's make...
SUPER SUSHI

Seafood is freely available along the Japanese coasts, rice flourishes in the fertile south of Japan, while nori seaweed grows mainly in the warm waters around Kyushu Island.

WHAT YOU NEED:

FOR THE SUSHI RICE:

340g short- or medium-grain rice
1 small piece of dried nori seaweed
2 teaspoons sugar

3 tablespoons rice vinegar (or mild cider vinegar)
½ teaspoon salt

FOR THE FILLING:

2 eggs
1 tablespoon soy sauce
1 teaspoon oil
¼ cucumber
1 carrot
¼ white daikon radish
a few curly endive lettuce or sorrel leaves
10 sheets dried roasted nori seaweed

2–3 teaspoons green Japanese horseradish paste (wasabi)

◁ To make this cone of sushi, you don't even need a sushi mat. You can just roll it in your hands.

1 Wash the rice and drain it in a sieve. Put it in a saucepan. Add 450ml water and the nori. Bring it to the boil over a low heat. Boil for 2 minutes in bubbling water.

3 Meanwhile, heat the vinegar in a small saucepan. Add the sugar and salt and stir until both have dissolved. Put the rice into a wide bowl and stir in the vinegar mixture. Allow to cool until you can touch the rice. Place a damp cloth over the bowl.

4 Crack the eggs into a cup. Stir in 1 tablespoon soy sauce. Heat the oil in a non-stick frying pan. Add the egg mixture and make an omelette. Take it out, let it cool, then cut it into strips.

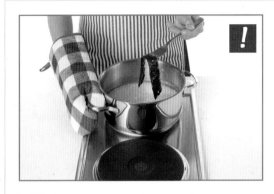

2 Fish out the nori. Turn the heat to very low and cover the saucepan. Simmer the rice for about 20 minutes. Stir from time to time. Turn off the heat and take off the lid. Cover the saucepan with a clean teatowel, replace the lid, and allow to stand for 10 minutes.

5 Wash and trim the carrot and radish. Cut both into slices, then into thin strips. Cook the carrot strips for 2 minutes in boiling water so they are still crunchy. Drain. Wash lettuce or sorrel, pat dry and tear into small pieces. Cut the nori sheets into fourths.

6 Hold a nori piece in your hand. Place on top 1 teaspoon sushi rice, cucumber strips, salad shreds, omelette and vegetable strips, and a little wasabi. Roll up the sheet to form a cone. Serve with soy sauce.

let's make...
FRIED TOFU

Tofu is a favourite meal of Buddhist monks, who eat no meat. Today it is a popular food all over Japan; especially in Kyoto, the town of 1,500 Buddhist temples.

WHAT YOU NEED:

SERVES 4 PEOPLE:

500g tofu
4 tablespoons flour
2 eggs
60g sesame seeds
6 tablespoons oil

FOR THE SAUCE:

120ml soy sauce
6 tablespoons rice vinegar
1 teaspoon ground pepper
a pinch of chilli powder
2 teaspoons sugar

◁ Hurray! Today is tofu day! Once a week, we eat tofu. Each time we use a different recipe: fried tofu, tofu in a soup or tofu grilled as a kebab.

WHAT DOES *tofu* TASTE LIKE?

Tofu has little flavour of its own, but it picks up the flavour of the other ingredients in the same dish or of a sauce. Vegetarians often use tofu instead of meat.

1 Cut the tofu into 12mm-thick slices. Cut the slices into strips, about 25mm by 50mm. **!**

2 Put the flour on a deep plate. Crack the eggs on to a second plate and beat them with a fork. Spread out the sesame seeds on a third plate.

3 Turn the tofu first in the flour, then in the egg, and finally in the sesame seeds, so it is covered in seeds all over, on both sides. In a small bowl, combine all the ingredients for the sauce.

4 Heat the oil in a wide frying pan until it is hot but has not yet started smoking. Add the tofu strips and fry them for 2–3 minutes. Turn them with a wooden spoon and fry the other side for 2–3 minutes. Serve with the sauce.

USING tofu

Tofu goes well with other foods. You can even use it in Western recipes, for example to make burgers or in meat pies.

MY TIP

Tofu does not keep very well. Eat it on the day you buy it, or keep it in some cold water in the fridge and eat the next day.

let's make...
SASHIMI

Sashimi means 'raw seafood'. Fish is perfectly safe to eat raw, if it is of good quality and very fresh. And Japan, with its long coastlines, has no shortage of fresh fish and seafood.

▽ I like all kinds of fish. My Mum says fish is brain food. Apparently it has lots of omega-3 oils in it and so it makes you intelligent too.

WHAT YOU NEED:

SERVES 4 PEOPLE:

1 small carrot
1 small piece of radish (about 50mm)
1 small piece of cucumber (about 50mm)
1 small unwaxed lemon
some coriander leaves or flat-leafed parsley
450g very fresh salmon fillet (alternatively use a mixture of very fresh salmon fillet, very fresh tuna fillet, cooked and peeled king prawns, and fresh scallops)

4 roasted nori sheets
4 teaspoons wasabi paste
10 tablespoons soy sauce

HOW CAN I TELL IF fish is fresh?

<u>Whole fish should have:</u>
• moist, slippery skin • scales firmly attached to the body • bright, moist gills • firm flesh • clear eyes • a fresh smell
<u>Fish fillets or steaks should have:</u> • firm flesh • a clear and even colour (white or red) • a moist look • a fresh smell

1 Peel the carrot, cucumber and radish. Trim the ends. Scrape out the cucumber seeds. Cut all into thin, finger-long strips. Scrub the lemon under hot water and pat it dry. Cut it with its zest into thin slices. Wash the coriander and pat it dry.

2 Wash all the fish and seafood you are using under cold water. Pat dry with kitchen paper. Cut the fish across the fibres, into 12mm-thick slices. If you are using king prawns, cut them into smaller pieces.

3 Cut the nori sheets into small pieces. In a cup or small bowl, stir the wasabi into the soy sauce. Pour the mixture into four small bowls. Arrange all other ingredients decoratively on a serving dish.

4 To eat the sashimi, hold a slice of fish (or a piece of scallop or prawn) with your chopsticks, dip it into the spiced soy sauce and enjoy.

How we celebrate in
JAPAN

People in Japan celebrate many national holidays, as well as some introduced from other cultures.

In Japan, holidays are celebrated to honour the Japanese emperor, to show respect for the elderly and the deceased, and to celebrate nature and the arrival of spring. Children, too, have their own special days.

New Year holiday

Shogatsu is Japan's most important national festival. In the days leading up to new year, people hold *bonekai* parties to 'forget the old year'. Then everyone stops work for a three-day holiday. Houses are thoroughly cleaned and decorated with pine, plum and bamboo twigs. People send postcards to arrive on 1 January, and children receive presents.

Families gather to spend time together. They share a meal of soba – long buckwheat noodles that symbolise long life. They watch popular TV shows. As the New Year arrives, the bells ring out in Buddhist temples across the country. They chime 108 times, because Buddhists believe that people have to overcome 108 worldly desires. Many people stay up to watch the sunrise at temples and other beauty spots. On New Year's Day, people eat *osechi-ryori*. This food consists of neatly prepared delicacies, all beautifully stacked in layers in lacquer boxes. The food is eaten with rice wine and a soup with rice dumplings. No one needs to do much cooking over the New Year holiday.

Bean-throwing ceremony

Setsubun is a traditional spring festival that is held on 3 or 4 February. In the past, people burned fish heads to drive away evil spirits. Today, they decorate a holiday tree with a sardine head, a clove of garlic or an onion. They scatter roasted 'happiness beans' in homes, and in religious shrines and temples. For good luck, people pick up and eat as many beans as they are years old.

Doll festival

At Hina Matsuri, parents wish their daughters a happy and successful life. This traditional doll festival is held on 3 March. Beautifully dressed doll models of the emperor, empress and their courtiers are displayed on shelves covered with red cloth. The display is often

◁ **Bon Odori** is a traditional summer dance festival enjoyed by people all over Japan. Originally the festivities thanked the Rice Paddock God for a good harvest. People dance to the rhythm of taiko drums.

CHERRY BLOSSOM TIME

The first cherry blossom, or sakura, marks the end of the bone-chilling winter. Every park with sakura trees is packed with people who celebrate together.

decorated with peach blossoms. The dolls can be precious family heirlooms, which are handed down from one generation to another. The dolls often have miniature furniture and other household items, and children offer them tiny rice cakes.

After the festival, each girl needs to put the dolls away quickly. If she doesn't, it is said, she will not get married for a long time.

Golden Week

Golden Week falls between 29 April and 5 May and includes several national holidays. Many Japanese people take their holidays during that week. Showa Day is 29 April; it was the birthday of Emperor Hirohito, or Showa, who ruled Japan during World War II (1939–1945). The next holiday is Constitution Day. It commemorates 3 May 1947, when Japan's

△ *Traditional dancers* perform in a street. Japanese dances include courtly and religious as well as theatrical dances.

democratic constitution was written. This is followed by Greenery, or Nature, Day on 4 May, when people celebrate the beauty of the natural world. The final holiday is Children's Day; it is celebrated on 5 May *(see page 28)*.

Star Festival

Tanabata, or Star Festival, celebrates the tale of two lovers who can only meet once a year, on 7 July, when two stars cross paths in the Milky Way. Today, people write wishes and poems on strips of coloured paper. They tie the papers to trees made from bamboo. Tanabata competitions are held around the country for the best decorations. In the city of Sendai, people make seven different kinds of paper decorations. Children sing a song about rustling bamboo leaves and stars.

Festival of Souls

Bon, or Obon, is a Buddhist festival. It is held in mid-July or August to celebrate the spirits of the ancestors. Bon is a time for decorating family graves. People also clean their homes and light fires to welcome in the spirits of the dead. They pray at their home altars and decorate these with paper lanterns. They also make food offerings. People dance to comfort the dead, and they float candle-lit lanterns to guide the spirits home on water.

△ *A samurai and a geisha figure* are two of the dolls at the Nihonmatsu Chrysanthemum Festival in October. The chrysanthemum is Japan's national flower, and 30,000 chrysanthemums decorate the festival dolls.

FESTIVAL LUNCHBOX

Bento lunchboxes (small lacquer boxes) are popular for eating on the go, at festivals or while travelling.

let's make...
SOBA NOODLE SOUP

We eat noodle dishes at many festivals. The longer the noodles, the better – they are symbolic of a long life. So we like to serve them to older relatives, and wish them many more years.

▽ Oodles of noodles! In Japan it's OK to eat noodles with a lot of slurping…

WHAT YOU NEED:

SERVES 4 PEOPLE:

2 eggs
50g baby leaf spinach
  or other tender leaf
  vegetables
1 small carrot
2 spring onions
1 sheet nori seaweed
450g soba noodles
1½ litres dashi stock
  (see page 41)
light soy sauce for
  flavouring

WHAT'S THIS: soba?

Real soba noodles are very long and thin, and they're made from buckwheat, a type of cereal. In Japan, we call all thin noodles *soba*, even if they're not made from buckwheat. Thick noodles are called *udon*.

1 Pierce each egg once with a skewer. Put the eggs in a saucepan with boiling water and boil them hard for 8 minutes. Refresh the eggs under cold running water, then peel them. Allow to cool, then slice the eggs.

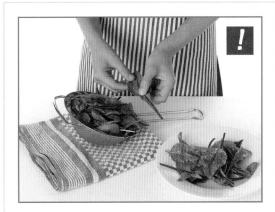

2 Wash the spinach; throw away any wilted leaves. Cut the spinach into strips. Peel the carrot; cut it into very thin slices. Wash and trim the spring onions, then cut them into thin slanted rings. Cut the nori into very thin strips.

3 In a large saucepan, bring plenty of water to the boil. Add the noodles and cook for about 5 minutes.

4 In another saucepan, heat the dashi. Add the vegetables and cook for 2 minutes. Add a little soy sauce. Drain the noodles in a sieve and divide them between four soup bowls.

5 Ladle the soup over the noodles. Add the egg and nori strips. Serve and slurp!

let's make...
TAMAGOYAKI

These rolled omelettes are popular at all occasions, for festivals and everyday eating, too. They are also delicious cold, so they are ideal for lunchboxes or a quick afternoon snack.

▽ Tamagoyaki are perfect for Japanese-style picnic boxes. We also take along sushi and pickles, especially pickled ginger. Then we go to a park, sit down on a large blanket, and enjoy our Japanese 'takeaway'.

WHAT YOU NEED:

SERVES 4 PEOPLE:

8 eggs
5 tablespoons dashi
   (or chicken stock)
2 teaspoons sugar
4 teaspoons soy sauce
3 tablespoons green parts
   of spring onions, finely
   chopped
a little oil for frying

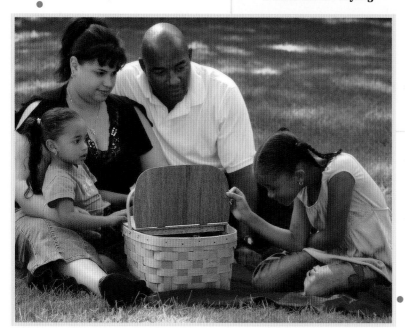

HOW WE COOK THE <u>omelette</u>

In Japan, we use a square frying pan to make tamagoyaki. This makes it easier to shape the omelette into regular long rolls.

MY TIP

These omelette rolls are perfect for *bento*, which is what we call our lunchboxes.

1 Crack the eggs into a bowl and beat them with a fork. Stir in the dashi, sugar, soy sauce and the spring onion pieces.

2 Heat a little oil in a deep omelette pan over a low heat. Keep the heat really low, so the sugar in the mix does not make the omelette burn. **!**

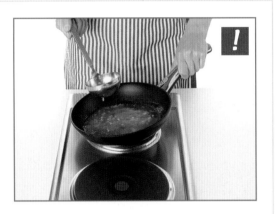

3 Put one ladle of the egg mixture into the frying pan. Turn the pan from side to side, so the bottom of the pan gets covered with egg mixture.

4 When the egg has set, carefully roll up the omelette from one side towards the centre. Leave it in the pan.

5 Put some more oil in the frying pan, and add more egg. Slip the egg under the finished omelette too. Fry until it is almost but not completely set. **!**

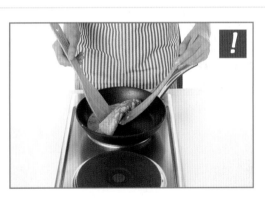

6 Now roll this second omelette around the first one, to make it into a thicker roll.

7 Continue frying more omelettes and rolling them around finished ones until all the egg is used up. Take the omelette roll out of the pan. Place it on a bamboo roll or a clean kitchen towel and flatten it. Once it has cooled, cut it into 25mm slices and serve. **!**

How we celebrate at home in JAPAN

A part from the national and regional festivities, there are also many events that families celebrate privately. In Japan, reaching a particular age is an important reason to celebrate.

Seven-Five-Three Festival

In Japan, a child's third, fifth and seventh birthdays are the most important birthdays in his or her life. On the weekend closest to 15 November, the Seven-Five-Three Festival, or Shichi-Go-San, takes place. On this day, parents take their sons between the ages of three and five, and their daughters between the ages of three and seven, to a local Shinto shrine. Here, they pray that their children will stay healthy and have a long life.

Children wear their best clothes, which may be Japanese or Western in style. Traditional outfits include silk kimonos with sandals or matching slippers for girls, and jackets and *hakama* (folded, skirt-like trousers) for boys.

Children's Day

From the end of April until Children's Day, on 5 May, colourful carp-shaped windsocks called *koinobori* flutter in the wind all over Japan. Once this holiday was a celebration just for boys, but now girls celebrate too. The koi carp is a symbol of strength. This is because an ancient Chinese legend tells the story of a carp that swam up a waterfall and turned into a dragon.

Warrior dolls and helmets are on display to symbolise strength. Some homes place the armour and weapons of samurai warrior models in special niches. Boys wear paper helmets and eat sweet rice cakes with their families.

Coming of Age Day

When young people turn twenty in Japan, they officially become adults and have new duties. This is known as *Seijin hi*, or Coming of Age Day. It is a national holiday on the second Monday in January. Everyone celebrates at the same time, even if their birthday is not on that day. The boys wear kimonos or suits, and the girls wear kimonos with white fur collars. They visit Shinto shrines and have their photo taken.

◁ **For the Coming of Age Day**, girls wear special *furisode kimonos* and *zori* slippers. They go out in town and celebrate with their friends who have also become adults that day.

Mother's Day

Mother's Day, or *Haha no hi*, is celebrated on the second Sunday in May. Children give their mother red carnations or other gifts. They help out with chores at home and cook a meal, or go out as a family to a restaurant. At school, many children make special gifts for their mother or draw a picture.

Father's Day falls on the third Sunday in June. Some schools hold special Sunday classes, so that busy fathers can see first-hand how their children are doing at their studies.

The tea ceremony

The traditional Japanese tea ceremony, or *chaji*, has many formal rules. Learning how to prepare and serve tea properly can take years.

The host dresses in formal clothes and prepares and serves the tea in a special tea house, which often stands in the garden. The type of tea used is powdered green leaves called *maccha*. The powder is stirred with a bamboo whisk. The ceremony includes many ritual gestures, both for the host and for the guest, which have to be learned.

Weddings

Weddings usually take place in the spring or the autumn. Although many people are not very religious today, the wedding ceremonies

▽ **Chashitsu** is a room that has been specially designed for the tea ceremony. The host prepares for days for the ceremony. He or she makes sure that everything is perfect when the guests arrive.

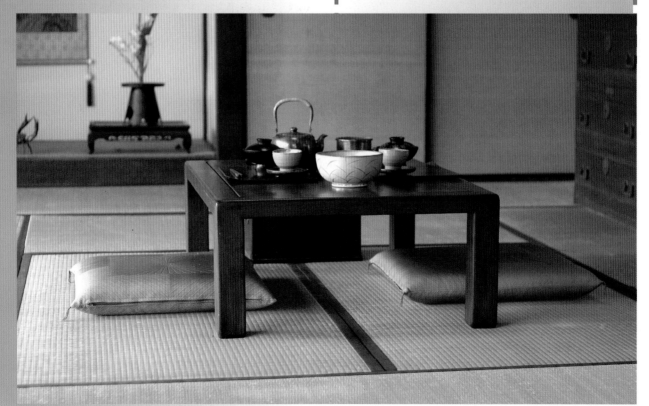

are quite formal. They follow Buddhist, Shinto or Christian traditions. The couple say their marriage vows, drink sake and exchange their glasses. The guests join them for the wedding reception. They bring money gifts for the couple in red envelopes.

Christmas

Aside from Buddhist and Shinto festivals, some people also celebrate Christian holidays such as Christmas Day. They set up Christmas trees in their homes, and parents give their children presents. For some Buddhists, a monk called Hotei-osho comes in place of the Western Father Christmas and brings the presents.

△ *This Japanese snowman* looks like a Christmas tree. Many people also decorate the outside of their homes with Christmas lights.

◁ *Red and white* are lucky colours in Japan. The bride and groom make sure they wear something that is red. The food that is served at the wedding banquet is also red in colour.

let's make...
SUKIYAKI

This dish is a bit like a Western fondue. It's prepared at the table. For special occasions, people sit around the table and cook their own food.

▽ A gas burner or a tea warmer with tea-tree lights is perfect for keeping the frying pan hot while we cook our food.

WHAT YOU NEED:

SERVES 4 PEOPLE:

500g fillet of beef
125g glass noodles
2 bunches spring onions
3 large carrots
375g fresh shiitake
  mushrooms
250g tofu
120ml soy sauce
180ml vegetable stock
1 tablespoon beef dripping
  (or cooking oil)
    3 teaspoons sugar
    white pepper
    your favourite
    dipping sauces

HOW DO I EAT <u>sukiyaki?</u>

Put a slice of meat in the stock and cook it for 5 minutes, then push it to the edge of the frying pan. Pour in a little more stock. Add some of the other ingredients and cook for a few minutes. The sauce should only just cover the bottom of the pan. Everyone now picks out with chopsticks what they'd like to eat and dips the food in their favourite sauce. Continue cooking more meat and vegetables, and adding stock.

1 Wash the meat and pat it dry. Cut it into thin slices. Put the noodles into a bowl, pour boiling water over them, and leave them to soak.

2 Wash and trim the spring onions. Cut the white parts into thin, slanted rings. Cut the green parts into 50mm lengths, and cut these into matchsticks. Peel and chop the onion. Wipe the mushrooms clean with a damp cloth, then cut them into thick strips.

3 Drain the tofu and cut it into cubes. Drain the glass noodles. Leave them to stand. Stir the soy sauce into the stock. Set out all the ingredients. Put the dipping sauces into small bowls.

4 Heat the dripping or cooking oil in a wide frying pan on top of the stove. Sprinkle in the sugar and stir until it turns to caramel. Pour in a little of the soy stock – do this very carefully and from a distance! It could splatter and burn you. Keep the sauce hot on the gas burner.

let's make...
TEMPURA

For this festive dish we coat food in a very light batter. The batter is so light that you can see the colour of the vegetables underneath. We also cook fish and seafood this way.

▽ I sprinkle my tempura pieces with grated radish and dip them in a sauce of dashi *(see page 41)*, mirin and shoyu.

WHAT YOU NEED:

SERVES 4 PEOPLE:

200g peeled prawns
(with their tails intact)
400g broccoli
375g courgettes
375g fine French
beans
60g flour
oil for deep frying
2 egg yolks
300ml ice-cold
water
½ teaspoon salt
flour for coating

MY TIP

The secret of perfect tempura batter is not to mix it too vigorously. Don't ever use a blender to combine the ingredients – it makes the batter too smooth. Instead, put the ingredients in a bowl and gently stir them with chopsticks.

1 Cut the broccoli into smaller pieces. Slice the courgette and halve very large slices. Cut the ends off the beans, but leave them whole. Wash the prawns under cold water, drain them and pat them dry. Wash and trim the vegetables.

2 Bring plenty of water to the boil in a large saucepan. Briefly cook one vegetable at a time – broccoli for 4 minutes, courgettes 2 minutes, beans 5 minutes – all should still be crunchy. Lift out the half-cooked vegetables with a slotted spoon and rinse them under cold water. Drain. In a fondue pot, heat the oil for deep frying. Keep the oil hot over a flame.

3 Put all the vegetable pieces and prawns into a plastic bag, add the flour, and close. Shake well to coat everything with flour. Place all the pieces on a large plate.

5 To cook tempura, hold a prawn or vegetable with your chopsticks (or with a fork), dip them in the batter, then hold them into the hot fat. Take out after 1 minute. It's ready to eat, but be careful not to burn your mouth – it is very hot!

4 When you are ready to eat, make the batter. Combine the egg yolks, the ice-cold water, the flour and the salt *(see My Tip on the left)*. Put the batter into individual bowls so each person can cook their own tempura.

How we live in
JAPAN

People in Japan live mainly in the large cities, and the most important city is the capital, Tokyo. Aside from their home lives, school and the workplace are very important to people. Once, men were the only breadwinners, while women looked after the home and cared for children and the elderly. This is changing here as elsewhere.

The Japanese home

A traditional Japanese house is made of wood. It is supported by wooden posts. The floors are covered with a woven straw mat, called a *tatami*. People used to sleep on the floor on futons that can be rolled up and put away during the day to make a living room.

Today, most families live in houses or blocks of flats similar to those in the West. But they still have at least one room that is furnished with a tatami mat. Before entering a Japanese home, people take off their shoes and put on slippers.

Today, people only wear a *kimono* on special days. A kimono is a long silk robe that is tied at the waist with a wide belt called an *obi*. Children wear shorter kimonos called *yakuta*. Everyday clothes are casual and international in style.

People entertain friends mostly outside their homes because there is normally very little space for guests.

ALL ABOARD

At busy times, some underground trains in Tokyo get so crowded that special 'people pushers' called oshiya have to help push more people on to the trains before the doors close!

City life

Japan's cities are busy and crowded, but there are plenty of things to do in the cities. People visit beautiful gardens and parks, playgrounds, historic buildings, museums, theme parks, zoos and aquariums. Travel on the underground is quick and cheap. But the trains get very crowded at the start and the end of the working day. Eleven million people commute to work in Tokyo each day; they come on buses, trains and the underground.

Country life

Fewer than a quarter of all people in Japan live in the country. Life there is not as fast-paced as in the large cities and their suburbs. But life can be hard in the country too. Work in the fields is back-breaking. Many people from farming villages have to travel a long distance into towns and cities to find work so they can get by.

School classes in Japan's remote mountain and fishing villages often have very few pupils. Children also travel far to their nearest school, either on foot or by bus. But in small villages people know each other. They often stop for a chat and help each other in times of need. So people in villages are rarely lonely, and the elderly are often well cared for.

Life at school

Most children in Japan go to excellent state schools. Children start school the April before they are six years old. They spend three years in infant school and three in junior school, then they go on to a secondary school.

The main subjects at school are reading and writing, maths, science, social studies, music, crafts, physical education and home economics. There are 2,000 characters in the Japanese language, so learning to write is difficult. Many children also learn calligraphy. This is the art of writing beautiful letters with a brush and ink. Pupils take *bento* lunchboxes from home. These include tasty foods, such as sushi or omelettes called *tamagoyaki*.

▽ **Students learn** to play Western musical instruments such as violins. Today, they also learn about Japan's own musical traditions. Playing ancient instruments, such as the *koto* (zither), *shakuhachi* (flute) and *taiko* (drum), is also part of their lessons.

△ **Shinkansen** are fast Japanese trains that connect the major cities. These were the first high-speed trains in the world, and they hold the world speed record of 577km per hour.

Time off

After a busy day at school, children have many activities to choose from. Some children join sports clubs to play baseball, basketball, martial arts, soccer, tennis or swimming. At home, they relax with video and computer games, and watch cartoons on TV. Family activities include hiking, cycling, skiing,

fishing and going to the beach. Sumo wrestling is Japan's national sport. People also enjoy going to festivals, visiting museums and parks, and admiring the cherry blossom in spring and leaf colours in autumn.

Meal times

Traditionally, the family used to sit around a low table on tatami mats. Each person picked up food from the serving dishes with their chopsticks and put them into their own bowl. Today, parents and children spend long hours at work and school. They have less time to prepare fresh food and eat more fast food.

let's make...
MISO SOUP

We eat miso soup almost every day – for breakfast, after school, and before other dishes at dinner. It is delicious and comforting, and it aids digestion.

▽ You can eat the leeks and tofu in this soup with chopsticks. But try eating the soup itself like that!

WHAT YOU NEED:

SERVES 4 PEOPLE:

150–175g Japanese tofu
2 thin leeks
a piece fresh ginger,
   about 18mm long
750ml dashi stock
4 tablespoons miso
   (soyabean paste)

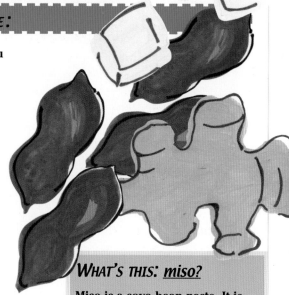

WHAT'S THIS: <u>miso?</u>

Miso is a soya bean paste. It is made from fermented soya beans or grains, such as rice. We use miso in many different dishes.

MY TIP

Dashi is the base for many soups and sauces in Japan – so make a larger amount and freeze it.

1 Wash the tofu under cold water and cut it into 25mm cubes. Wash the leek, cut off all wilted leaves. Cut the leeks into very thin rings or strips and wash it again. **!**

3 Heat the dashi stock in a large saucepan, but do not let it boil. Put the miso paste into a bowl. Stir a little stock into the miso. **!**

2 Peel the ginger, then grate it finely. Squeeze it with your fingers. Save the juice and throw the ginger away.

! How do I make _dashi_ stock?

To make four portions of dashi, buy a piece of konbu (a dried seaweed) of about 150mm by 150mm. Wipe it with a clean cloth, but do not wash it with water. Cut the konbu into wide strips, and place these in a saucepan.

Add 1 litre water and bring it to the boil over a medium heat. As soon as the water starts to bubble, take the saucepan off the heat. Lift out the konbu.

Stir the bonito flakes into the water and return to the boil. Take the saucepan off the heat. Leave it for about 1–2 minutes, until the bonito flakes have sunk to the bottom of the pan.

Line a sieve with a fine cloth. Pour the dashi through the sieve. Continue as above, from Step 3.

4 Now add the miso–stock mixture to the rest of the dashi stock, a little at a time. Stir in the tofu, leeks and ginger juice. Serve hot.

let's make...
CHICKEN & EGG DOMBURI

This is a typical midweek meal. People often eat domburi after a bowl of miso soup, sometimes even for breakfast. It is a rice dish, with a topping of chicken and mushrooms.

▽ If you hold the bowl close to your mouth, you can make sure that none of this delicious food drops off your chopsticks.

WHAT YOU NEED:

SERVES 4 PEOPLE:

340g short-grain
   Japanese rice
salt
1 large boneless chicken
   breast, without skin
75g fresh shiitake
   mushrooms
1 bunch spring
   onions
240ml strong chicken stock
6 tablespoons light
   soy sauce
6 eggs

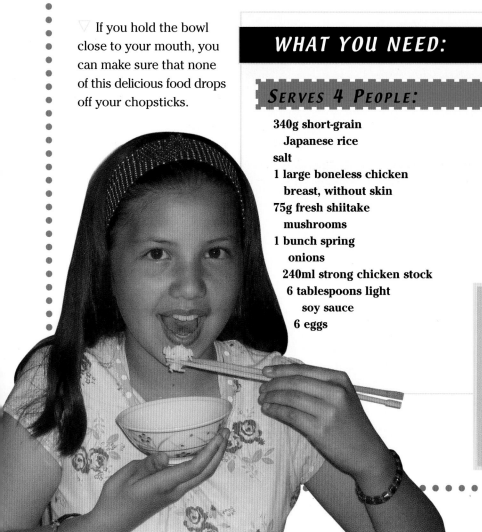

WHAT'S THIS: domburi?

Domburi is the Japanese word for bowl, because we always eat this dish out of a bowl. The chicken and egg topping is also known as *oyako domburi*. That means 'mother and child domburi'. Why? Because it contains chicken – and egg!

1 Put the rice into a saucepan of lightly salted boiling water. Cook for about 15 minutes. Drain and cover the pan to keep the rice warm. **!**

2 Wash the chicken under cold water. Pat it dry with kitchen paper. Cut the chicken into very thin strips. **!**

4 Heat the stock in a wok, add the soy sauce, the chicken strips, mushrooms and spring onions. Cook everything for about 3 minutes. **!**

3 Cut off any wilted parts from the mushrooms. Wipe the mushrooms clean with moist kitchen paper. Wash and trim the spring onions. Cut the onions into very thin slanted rings.

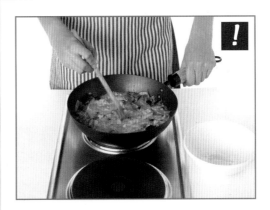

5 Crack the eggs into a small bowl and beat them with a fork. Pour the mixture into the wok. Cook over a gentle heat for 2 minutes, until the egg mix has set (becomes firm).

6 Divide the rice between individual bowls. Spoon the chicken–egg mixture over the top and serve.

let's make...
GREEN TEA ICE CREAM

Hokkaido, in northern Japan, has many dairy farms. This delicious and refreshing dessert combines milk and cream with the best Japanese tea, from Shizuoka.

▽ This delicious ice cream is a dessert choice in many Japanese snack bars and restaurants. And now I can make it myself!

WHAT YOU NEED:

SERVES 4 TO 6 PEOPLE:

2 tablespoons maccha green tea powder
40ml hot water
2 egg yolks
100ml milk
2 tablespoons sugar
¾ cup double cream

WHAT'S THIS: green tea?

Green tea is the most popular drink in Japan. Tea farms are everywhere, especially in the Shizuoka area. Maccha powder is made by grinding steamed and dried green tea leaves into a powder, using a stone mortar.

1 Put the green tea powder and the hot water into a bowl. Stir well, then set the bowl to one side. **!**

2 Put the egg yolks into a small high saucepan. Beat them with a fork until they are smooth. Stir in the milk and the sugar. **!**

3 Heat the egg and milk mixture over a very low heat. Stir all the time, until the mixture thickens. **!**

4 Put plenty of ice-cold water and ice cubes into a large bowl. Place the saucepan with the egg mixture into this bowl. Stir in the tea powder. Whisk the cream until it is stiff.

5 Gently stir the stiff cream into the egg and tea mixture, using a figure-eight motion. When all is combined, put the mixture into the freezer for at least 3 hours. Serve cold.

How do I make green tea?

People make and drink different teas at different temperatures in Japan. To make maccha tea, put 1 teaspoon of powder into your tea pot. Add 1.5l hot water at 100°C (gas mark ½) and stir well with a bamboo tea whisk.

Look it up
JAPAN

bento a Japanese lunchbox with compartments for several different dishes, often including sushi and tamagoyaki

dashi a Japanese broth or stock, the base for miso and other soups and sauces

green tea the typical Japanese tea; it is drunk daily and served during the tea ceremony; it is also an ingredient in many dishes

kimono the traditional silk dress worn by Japanese women; there are many versions

miso a traditional food made from fermented soya beans and other ingredients; miso is a part of miso soup, which is drunk before meals or for breakfast

omikuji a paper fortune that can be bought at a Shinto temple

shinkasen the Japanese high-speed train, known as the bullet train in the West; it was the first high-speed train in the world, and it is the holder of the world speed record

Shinto the main Japanese religion

soba long, thin buckwheat noodles – a symbol of longevity, or a long life

sushi a rolled food made from vinegared rice and vegetables or seafood, often wrapped in nori seaweed

tamagoyaki a Japanese rolled omelette, made from several layers of set egg

torii an entrance gate before a Shinto shrine, sometimes it seems to be floating in water

tofu a beancurd made from soya beans; part of many vegetarian meals in Japan

Find out more
JAPAN

Books to read

Case, Robert
Countries of the World: Japan
Evans Brothers, 2005

Messager, Alexandre, and Duffet, Sophie
**We Live in Japan (Kids Around the
    World)**
HNA Books, 2007

Reynolds, Jeff
Japan (A to Z)
Children's Press, CT, 2005

Wiltshire, Diane, and Huey, Jeanne
**Japan for Kids: The Ultimate Guide
    for Parents and Their Children**
Kodansha International, 2000

Web sites to check out

www.japan-guide.com
A travel web site with a good A–Z section
on the arts, culture, food, history, and more

http://web-japan.org/kidsweb
A children's web site including recipes,
culture notes, legends, and 'cool stuff'

**www.japaneselifestyle.com.au/culture/
culture.html**
All about Japanese culture, with entries
on geishas, festivals, calligraphy, and more

www.japan-guide.com/e/e620.html
All about Japanese food, with information
on ingredients and recipes

**www3.nationalgeographic.com/places/
countries/country_japan.html**
The National Geographic magazine's
site on Japan

Index

JAPAN